A History of Plumbate Ware

By BERTHA P. DUTTON

Preface

FROM December 3 to March 3, 1938-1939, the School of American Research and Museum of New Mexico conducted archaeological excavations near the village of Tajumulco, in the department of San Marcos, in southwestern Guatemala. The expedition was in charge of the writer and Miss Hulda R. Hobbs of the museum staff. Miss Barbara H. L. Loomis, of Colorado Springs, Colorado, served as student assistant.

During the season, the small ruin site was cleared; the major pyramid and about two-thirds of the main plaza were excavated, together with platforms, terraces, courts, and miscellaneous features of approximately half the area of the main ruin; and preliminary clearing of the second largest mound and adjoining lineaments was accomplished.

Excavation disclosed stone sculptures, many small artifacts, tombs, and some human remains. Compared with other findings, exclusive of the sculptured stones, there was a relative wealth of pottery. Of the seventy-four complete or restorable vessels recovered, it was determined that over fifty per cent was of a type known as *plumbate ware.* When this material was being studied, the problems concerning plumbate ware proved to be increasing rather than decreasing.*

Reprinted, with modified illustration captions, from *El Palacio*, vol. XLIX, nos. 10, 11, and 12, October-December, 1942.

*The Tajumulco material includes typical plumbate vessels and also atypical pieces. Therefore, the term "plumbate group" has been employed, encompassing *plumbate*, which meets the recognized standards of true plumbate ware, and *quasi-plumbate*, for specimens which have certain characteristics of plumbate ware, but do not meet all the requirements.

In a monograph prepared by the writer and Miss Hobbs on the *Excavations at Tajumulco* (now in press), there is presented a non-technical report on the ceramics of Tajumulco. Miss Anna O. Shepard, technician of the Carnegie Institution of Washington, D. C., kindly offered to assist with the pottery studies. In a forthcoming publication, she will give the results of her technical studies of Tajumulco specimens. Both reports necessitated a review of the history of plumbate ware.

This revealed the fact that this type of pottery has been known for over one hundred years. Various workers have described it, generally, and have given their personal ideas as to its possible constituents, its makers, and time and place of origin. One person has held certain opinions; the next one, contradictory views; while another has differed entirely. Instead of studying the material exhaustively, each investigator seems to have left that task for someone else. Throughout the years, more and more excavations have been conducted; archaeological procedures have been refined; new methods of approach and new technics have been perfected; and cultural correlations have become possible. All these accomplishments are brought out by the review of plumbate history.

It was felt that this history would be valuable if reproduced with the technical report, when precise information and proven facts would be given. However, since the writer had assembled the plumbate literature, it appeared feasible to avoid duplication of effort, and Miss Shepard urged the present publication *A History of Plumbate Ware*, to which she will refer in her technical report. All illustrations are of plumbate vessels excavated at Tajumulco.

President Van Buren of the United States of America, in the fall of 1839, sent John L. Stephens on a confidential mission to Central America. In the course of his travels, which continued through the following year,

Stephens visited many ruins of former Indian settlements, and made invaluable contributions to archaeological knowledge. Germane to this paper is the fact that he carried on studies and limited excavations at the ancient Mam Indian site, Zaculeu, near Huehuetenango, Guatemala.

Opening one of the mounds at Zaculeu, he came upon fragments of bones and two pottery vessels. His description of the pottery is brief: "The first of the two was entire when we discovered it, but, unfortunately, was broken in getting it out, though we obtained all the pieces. It is graceful in design, the surface is polished, and the workmanship very good. The last was already broken, and though more complicated, the surface is not polished."[1] Stephens illustrates these examples with sketches drawn by his artist companion, Frederick Catherwood.

From the illustration it is seen that the first vessel is a vase of the so-called lamp chimney form, with annular base, and relatively sharp shoulder. Grooves encircle the body, with a decorated panel—apparently incised designs —between them and the collared rim; and there is similar decoration on the base. Dr. A. V. Kidder, chairman of the division of historical research, of the Carnegie Institution of Washington, who has long engaged in and directed archaeological work in Middle America, says, in referring to this specimen: "I think there is no doubt that it was actually plumbate."[2] Here then, would be the earliest known reference to this type of pottery.

Forty years later, Dr. Crecencio Carrillo y Ancona, Bishop of Mérida in Yucatan, brought a piece of this ware to general attention. He described and illustrated[3] a vessel dug up in Puerto Progreso, near Mérida, which he recognized as being of peculiar character and which he described as a "fine enameled pottery."

1. Stephens, 1841, v. II, p. 231.
2. Kidder, Letter, 8-5-42.
3. Carrillo y Ancona, 1885 (study made in 1881).

PLUMBATE VASE

Lamp-chimney form with annular base

No. Eg11-10/28.*   *DS.* 9.0   *H.* 11.9.

Color: Orange-Cinnamon (13″ less gray to 15″)

*According to the catalog of the School of American Research, the site of Tajumulco is indicated by the code "Eg11." In the following legends only the specimen numbers will be given.

All measurements are in centimeters (*D.* = diameter, *DO* = diameter at orifice, *DS.* = diameter at shoulder, *GD.* = greatest diameter, *H.* = height). Capitalized color terms are those of Robert Ridgway (*Color Standards and Color Nomenclature,* 1912); when italicized, read by A. O. Shepard.

The explorations of Désiré Charnay in Mexico and Central America, from 1857-1882, yielded ceramic specimens which have since been determined as of the ware now under discussion. At Tenenepanco [Tenemepango] he dug up a number of tomb burials with funerary furniture[4] including "vasos de Tlaloc plumbate y con vasijas de forma *fine orange*."[5]

Marshall Saville, in 1882, explored an important tomb (No. 10) at Copán, and recovered four pieces of the ware with glaze-like luster.[6] With interest aroused, Saville then made a study of the geographical distribution of this ware, and listed the examples to be found in museums in America and in Europe. The results of his study were never published.[7] But he came to hold the opinion that this class of ceramics had originated in the region of Alta Verapaz, in Guatemala.

In 1895, Eduard Seler, of the Ethnographical Museum of Berlin, published an article,[8] in which he described the same ware as "apparently having an actual glaze." The specimens which he examined were from Alta Verapaz, for the most part, although he mentioned examples from Yucatan and Vera Cruz. At that time, Seler remarked: ". . . I have hitherto been unable to determine what kind of glaze is on these vessels, as rare and beautiful pieces were always concerned which could not be sacrified to chemical investigation. However, there is hope that Mr. Holmes, of Chicago, who at present is making a special

---

4. Charnay, 1887, pp. 169-170. These particular pieces appear to have been excavated in 1880.

5. Caso, Ms. note.

6. Merwin & Vaillant, 1932, p. 80, add the information that: "On the basis of a ladle and incense jar also in the tomb, these bowls connect with material from the vault of Stela M, which is the chief ceramic indicator for Copan II and bears the date 9-16-5-0-0. Another Plumbate jar was found in the general digging."

7. Upon the death of Saville, all of his papers passed into the hands of an heir who has been loath to let anyone examine them.

8. Seler, 1904, p. 107.

study of these vessels, will throw light on this question.[9] The broad geographic area within which these pieces are found proves that in them we have to deal with ware which was distributed by trade."[10]

Seler felt that the region in which these glazed vessels were made must have been that of the *tierra caliente* or close to it, where the tapir, parrot, coati, monkey, and toad of the hot country were known, as these are so frequently represented in the vessel forms. And he suspected Tabasco or Chiapas, in Mexico, as the source, remarking that, "In ancient times the former was a famous commercial center, and the industrial centers can not have been far from there."[11]

Carl Lumholtz, while carrying on explorations in Mexico, in 1898, chanced to be present when a man in the city of Tepic, in the modern state of Nayarit, dug up a rich burial, with which was a remarkable example of this ware, decorated in the likeness of a turkey. Although the vessel was struck with full force of the man's pick, it was fractured only at the point of contact. Lumholtz had some fragments from the base of the jar analyzed by Professor Morris Loeb, of New York University, who determined that the smooth, glistening finish was not a glaze. The paste was found to contain very little carbon, whereas the slip contained a large amount of it. In discussing this pottery, Lumholtz said: ". . . There is reason to believe that a factory or factories of this kind of ware existed at some place in the Tierra Caliente of Guatemala, or southernmost Mexico, and that through commerce it reached the

9. Mr. Neil M. Judd, curator, division of archaeology, at the U. S. National Museum, who was W. H. Holmes' literary executor, reports that there is nothing among Holmes' manuscript notes which gives any information on this question. There are only a few memoranda relating to individual pieces of "glazed ware."

10. Seler, 1904, p. 109.

11. Seler, 1904, p. 110.

more northern tribes. So far, however, the locality has not been discovered."[12]

In 1900, Saville obtained two fine specimens of this ware from the ruins of Teotihuacan, in the valley of Mexico. And, a few years later, other examples were recovered from the same ruins. These are figured by Batres in his report on Teotihuacan published in 1906,[13] where he speaks of one vessel as having "reflections of bronzed metal, color of Barbedienne patina."

Although his references are rather general, Joyce, in his *Mexican Archaeology*, published in 1914, mentions specimens which are "often found to be coated with a leaden-coloured glaze hard enough to resist the point of a knife. This is of course an accidental earth-glaze, produced in firing by the action of the smoke or heat on the surface of the slip."[14]

Seler, in a report published in 1915, gave considerable discussion regarding this class of pottery. His description is as follows:

> [It] is distinguished by a coloring, sometimes more of a greenish tint at other times more gray and in places lead-like. In spots or fields of varying size this is replaced in a very characteristic fashion by a yellowish-red, and the vessels display a metallic polish, which gives the ware exactly the appearance of glazed pottery. Most are jar-like, with wide, short necks and as a rule are combined with an animal or human form in such a manner that the heads with full details project from the front of the jar, while limbs, wings and tail are shown, if at all, merely by bas-

12. Lumholtz, 1902, vol. II, p. 299. Seler, 1915, p. 583, adds the information that "the metallic shiny overlay is not harder but softer than the centre of the vessel wall; and it is not melted more readily but with greater difficulty than the interior of the wall of the vessel. Accordingly the smooth metallic glistening overlay resembling glazing is not an actual glazing. And [Franz] Heger has proved this to me also of the pottery from El Salvador now in the Vienna Museum."

13. Batres, 1906, Appendix.

14. Joyce, 1914, p. 194.

relief on the side of the bowl. And these vessels change also into the shape of an animal or a human being. On the other hand there occur jar and beaker-like shapes with a standing figure in full detail on the front, or else a face, or merely with a bas-relief apparently geometrical, or unornamented. Where only the head of a human being or animal in relief is placed on the front of the vessel, it is always hollow. This hollow interior is connected with the outer world by a hole under the chin.[15]

This work discloses the existence of this ware from Tula, Hidalgo, southward through Teotihuacan; Uexotla near Texcoco, D. F.; Zoncautla, Canton Coatepec, Ver.; Acapetlahuacan near Atlixco, and Atotonilco and Quimistlan, in Puebla; Suchilquitongo, Etla, Oaxaca; and Chinkultic, Comitan, Chiapas; to Guatemala, including Coban and Las Pacayas, Alta Verapaz; Chimaltenango; Finca Pompeya near Antigua; Buena Vista, Retalhuleu; Patulul, Solola; into Salvador.

In the distributional treatise, Seler gives detailed descriptions of numerous specimens of this ware, and his plates LXXVII-LXXXI illustrate many of them. He then states:

> In regard to the place of origin of these peculiar earthen vessels, so distinct in technique, outward appearance and in great part also in shapes, the view is quite generally held that they were produced in a quite limited area, whence they have spread by purchase or immigration over the whole country from Tepic to El Salvador. This theory seems to be contradicted, however, by one fact. . . . It is this: the objects represented on them indicate for some an origin in the neighborhood of the Maya countries, Central American Tierra caliente; while others carry representations of Mexican character. Among the first I place the tapir vessel (fig. 233). For the tapir is not a native of the vicinity of Mexico, and is apparently also absent on the Vera Cruz coast... Like that

---

15. Seler, 1915, p. 557. The translation used is that of Thompson & Richardson, 1939, vol. V, no. 14, p. 69.

PLUMBATE EFFIGY JAR—BIRD FORM

No. 10/2. *DS*. 8.4. *H*. 9.3. Color: *Between Ferruginous and Cinnamon-Rufous; where reduced, Dark Olive with metallic splotches; Cameo Brown*— (10' i, 21''' m, and 7" k).

of the tapir the home of the turkey, on the gala vessel of Tepic, is far from Central Mexico. For this ... is clearly not the ordinary *Meleagris gallopavo* well known to the Mexicans and bred by them, but ... the beautifully colored *Meleagris ocellata,* a native of Yucatan and the Antilles. These two animals (parrot, raccoon, jaguar and ape [monkey] complete the picture) indicate with tolerable certainty a Central American Tierra caliente land as the origin of this pottery. Walter Lehmann thinks it was El Salvador, because vessels with metallic polish are today offered for sale in El Salvador for a small sum of money. I have always been in favor of the Vera Paz and neighboring districts, because there I have found with comparative frequency plumbate[16] sherds. However, the present material does not seem to permit a more exact determination.[17]

Spinden, also in 1915, mentioned this ware as represented by specimens in Salvador. He spoke of it as "a peculiar kind of pottery which is known to have passed in trade to Toltec cities in the Valley of Mexico,"[18] and which he placed as post-Maya. He described the ware thus:

. . . Without regard to the character of the decoration it may be classified at once by a semi-vitreous glaze. The ware is hard, thin, and fine-grained. The surface has a slight but unmistakable gloss, varying in hue from dull green to dull orange. The greenish variety predominates and it is likely that the orange-colored specimens were subjected to a reducing flame. In no one of the many examples that have come to the attention of the writer does the surface appear to have become actually liquid. Instead a slight suffusion seems to have taken place when the pottery was being fired. This may have been due to the presence of lead in the clay. Although the finest examples of this ware probably antedate the Spanish epoch by several centuries still it is worthy of note that the same green-

16. The translators use the term *plumbate* to conform to modern usage (see: p. 69).

17. Seler, 1915, p. 583 (or Thompson & Richardson, 1939, vol. V, no. 14, pp. 79-80).

18. Spinden, 1915, p. 470.

ish and semi-vitreous surface is seen on post-Spanish products.

The suffused surface of this ware would not carry sizing or painted designs and as a result we find the ware decorated, first, by incised designs, second, by plastic designs. Special attention seems to have been paid to the development of shape as an esthetic whole. Vases with varied profiles are seen as well as long-necked bottles with the body gracefully modified by flutings. . . . It will be observed that when faces or animal figures are reproduced by modeling there are no signs of archaism. The heads are in the full round while minor details are often expressed in incised lines. The applied plastic decoration is freely and realistically treated, with headdresses, etc., on wing-like projections. A human head is sometimes shown in an animal mouth in accordance with a fashion inaugurated by the Maya. Necklaces and other decorative objects are frequently worn by animals. The incised patterns are characterized by curvilinear motives of serpentine origin and by cross hatching. The figures of the best period are not particularly grotesque but this quality increases as we approach the Spanish epoch and in post-Spanish work we have a hodge podge of grotesque features put together without rhyme or reason.

This semi-vitreous ware seems to have been peculiar to the western half of Salvador and perhaps the adjacent portions of Guatemala. Since the glaze is probably dependent upon a natural quality of the clay rather than an added ingredient its locality should be capable of exact determination. It seems to have passed far and wide in trade.[19]

In his contribution to the Holmes Anniversary Volume, published in 1916, Saville challenged Spinden's placement of this ware in the post-Maya epoch, on the basis of his studies of material recovered from Tomb 10 at Copán, attributed to the best period of that site. There, he said, "the ware is of respectable antiquity, so far as remoteness from the Spanish period of occupancy is concerned. We have never seen any specimens that in any way are to be

---

19. Spinden, 1915, pp. 470-472.

QUASI-PLUMBATE JAR

No. 10/51. *DS.* 15.4. *H.* 17.0. Color: mottled—primary slip,
Orange-Cinnamon; secondary slip, *between Ferruginous and Kaiser
Brown and Cinnamon-Rufous; Dark Olive around crazing lines*—
(13″ less gray, 9′ j. 11′, 21‴ m).

regarded as resembling a Spanish type of decoration." Saville then concluded that "the ware should be considered as the product of some local tribe or clan which developed this particular type of ceramic art. Whether the place of origin is Salvador or Guatemala is at present undetermined, but future research in this important part of Central America should elucidate the problem."[20] In the same article, Saville described a "glaze-ware" whistling vessel collected in the department of Cortés, Honduras, in the Río Ulua region.[21]

The decade from 1916 to 1926 is represented by a paucity of information regarding this ware. However, Dr. S. G. Morley says that he may be the one who began to indicate this pottery as *plumbate ware,* for he was referring to it thus, by 1922—perhaps a year or two prior to that. His appellation was based on the external appearance—the glossy, metallic, lead-like sheen and hard surface. His use was only verbal.[22]

Seler-Sachs, in 1922, reported on pottery of this type from Los Tuxtlas, Vera Cruz.[23] In 1925, Ricketson found an excellent specimen of this pottery—a jar—in the débris of the Caracol at Chichen Itza.[24] Lothrop, in 1926, pointed out that Nicoya Polychrome vessels appear to be related to "the Plumbate or Glazed Ware, which probably centers in Salvador or Guatemala."[25] Here, apparently for the first time, the word "plumbate" was used in a published account, designating this long known ware. In the same year, Vaillant mentioned plumbate in his report.[26]

That this terminology rested on no substantial analyses of the constituents of the ware is indicated in Lothrop's

---

20. Saville, 1916, p. 424.
21. Saville, 1916, p. 425.
22. Morley, Personal Conversation, 6-26-42.
23. Seler-Sachs, 1922, Pl. 6, 34.
24. Ruppert, 1935, p. 107 and fig. 128a.
25. Lothrop, 1926, p. 115.
26. Vaillant, 1926, p. 272, quoted by Morley.

PLUMBATE EFFIGY VASE—ANTHROPOMORPHIC

No. 10/54. *GD.* 10.0 *H.* 17.0. Color: *Gray and dark blue-gray;*
orange on features and incising; interior reduced.

statement: "This class of pottery is distinguished primarily by the slight suffusion, apparently accidental, which has produced a semi-vitrified surface, an action due perhaps to the presence of lead in the clay."[27] In commenting on its wide distribution, he mentioned pieces of plumbate pottery from the Ulua valley in Honduras, from the shores of Lake Nicaragua, and even from the province of Chiriqui in Panama. Referring to the Copán discovery, mentioned above, he said that this "establishes the fact that they [vessels of plumbate ware] were objects of trade as early as the fifth or sixth century A. D."[28]

About the same time, Lothrop inspected the Batres Jáuregui collection of pottery from Finca Arévalo, a part of the site later designated as Kaminaljuyú,[29] in which he identified specimens of "plumbate ware with late types of design;"[30] the design was apparently contemporaneous with stone carvings of Mayan style.

During the field season of 1925-1926, of the [University of Pennsylvania] Museum Central American expedition in Guatemala and Salvador, an effort was made to determine the source of the clay from which plumbate "or glazed ware" was manufactured, as this pottery was found in some quantity in the vicinity of Suchitoto, Salvador. Lothrop said:

> . . . Information was obtained which indicates that this ware did come from the Suchitoto region[31] and not from Guatemala as has been supposed by some. In Suchitoto today there are many potters. The men have adopted the Spanish technique, work on a wheel, stain their ware with copper, and glaze it with lead; the women work entirely by hand, though in a differ-

27. Lothrop, 1926, pp. 115-116.

28. Lothrop, 1926, p. 116.

29. In the Quiché language, this means "Hills of the Dead." *See* Carnegie Institution of Washington, *News Service Bulletin*, vol. 4, no. 6, 1936-1938, p. 55.

30. Lothrop, 1926a, p. 167.

31. Tajumulco is c. 350 k. in an air line from Suchitoto.

ent manner from that employed in eastern Salvador. Inquiry among these potters as to the existence of a "clay which assumed a natural glaze when fired" brought forth the answer that such a clay had been used long ago but that none knew whence it came. More specifically, an old woman said that her grandmother had used such a clay and had obtained it near the Valle Juancora. Then she added without prompting that this clay was peculiar, for it assumed either a gray-green or orange color according to the temperature at which it was fired. This, of course, is a faithful description of plumbate ware, and shows the general region from which the clay came, even though the exact spot remains to be determined.[32]

Shortly afterward, in another article, Lothrop wrote of the wide distribution of plumbate ware, and said that it "has proved a puzzling problem to the archaeologist, for its distribution is greater than any other New World pottery type, its stylistic affinities are variable, and its manufacture covered more than a thousand years."[33]

At that time, Lothrop had examined nearly a hundred examples of plumbate pottery from El Salvador alone, most of which came from the Pipil region in the center of the republic. He remarked, "The place where plumbate ware was manufactured has never been determined, but the great number (comparatively speaking) of vessels found in central Salvador suggest that it was made there."[34] The fact that certain varieties of plumbate ware were present in the upper levels of cultural remains in Salvador, and associated with Toltec remains, shows that this pottery was being made in relatively recent times.

For his doctoral dissertation, presented at Harvard University in 1927, George Vaillant prepared a report on "The Chronological Significance of Maya Ceramics." In this work he discussed plumbate ware to some extent and mentioned its known distribution up to that date. A few

32. Lothrop, 1927, pp. 26-27.
33. Lothrop, 1927a, p. 204.
34. Vaillant, 1927, p. 94.

PLUMBATE EFFIGY JAR—*Tepescuinte*

No. 10/6. *DS.* 6.1. *H.* 8.5. Color: *uniform thin orange olive-gray on one arm, touches "mud-crack" red; interior reduced.*

new observations were made, but no proof was offered for their authenticity. For instance, Vaillant stated:

> The basal paste of Plumbate Ware is a fine-grained extremely hard clay with a thin slip of the basal paste diluted. This clay is built up in vessels with uniformly thin walls. The firing seems to be more intense than is customary for aboriginal pottery north of the Panama Canal. The normal shade of the slip varies from grey to an olive drab. When subjected to an unusually fierce heat, the pottery takes on a bright red hue. Under fire the clay seems to sweat out particles that give a glazed effect to the surface of finished vessels. Possibly this luster has its origin in the presence of lead in the glaze. While the potters undoubtedly intended to make such vessels, it is very probable that they knew only the clays that would give this iridescence and did not have the sagacity to make mixtures chemically that would give an analogous effect.[35]

He spoke of the variety of forms, and said that almost every shape could be "reproduced in Salvador. This centralization of forms, coupled with the presence of clays which fuse into a luster, make Salvador in all probability the source for Plumbate."[36]

One of his observations was that, "The small size and the relative eccentricity of the forms confirm the conclusion that Plumbate is almost exclusively an art ware."[37] He then presented a classification, which is as follows:

1. Simple vessels, bottles and bowls.
2. Vessels with elements fitted to give a zoomorphic appearance.
3. Vessels (a) the bodies of which have been altered by modelling to meet the exigencies of zoomorphosis.
   (b) with a specialized form of pear-shaped body with realistically treated feet and other appendages.
   (c) with complicated incised patterns, the accen-

---

35. Vaillant, 1927, p. 93.
36. Vaillant, 1927, p. 94.
37. Vaillant, 1927, p. 94.

tuation of which is often accomplished by breaking up into terraces the original simple outline of the vessel.[38]

Concluding the chapter on plumbate ware, Vaillant stated:

Some of the vessels considered in Type 1 might be found in association with jars of Type 3-c. Yet in the sequence of styles described above there seems to be a transition from simple to complicated forms. The common occurrence of Plumbate in Toltec sites and its rarity in Old Empire Maya sites is significant. . . . The wide distribution of vases representing the Toltec divinity Tlaloc and the occurrence of vases with annular bases also argue for the trading of Plumbate at the time of the first Nahua invasions. . . . the Tlaloc vases must indicate the actual presence of Toltecs to superintend their manufacture. There is a very modern flavor to the fabrication of these vases, chiefly, it would seem, for export. . . .[39]

Specimens found in Tomb 10 at Copán, mentioned above, were identified by Vaillant as being of plumbate Types 1 and 2. The tomb, he said, was probably constructed at the close of the fifth century A.D., which "would seem to throw the invention of this ware into times coeval with the Maya Early Empire."[40] Later, in recapitulating his findings, he stated:

The appearance of Plumbate Ware in wide distribution throughout Toltec lands makes a strong contact likely between the Salvadorenos and the Nahua before the eleventh century when the Toltec Empire probably collapsed, although there may have been several intermediary nations. Whether there would have been an infiltration of Toltec religious elements is hard to say, but Toltec pressure must have squeezed up the people between the Nahua and Salvador, so that there was no great distance for such elements to be diffused. The break-up of Copan and the loss of its cultural inspiration in Salvador might have been

38. Vaillant, 1927, p. 94.
39. Vaillant, 1927, pp. 105-106.
40. Vaillant, 1927, p. 260.

[19]

PLUMBATE BOWL

No. 10/14. DO. 17.5. H. 6.7. Color: *Pale blue-gray, orange and small areas of Mouse Gray.*

compensated for by the infiltration of Nahua ideas from the west. In time the potters might have been so deadened by Nahua contact that they lost interest in producing the fine polychrome pottery of the earlier days. Single families might have, in a reduced and degenerate way, produced a shell of the Maya decoration, which would account for the transitional forms. At some time between the downfall of Copan and the conquest, true Nahua like the Pipil might have come in.[41]

Discussing the Pipil, Vaillant said: "According to native traditions, these people were an offshoot from the great Toltec Empire, which collapsed in the eleventh century, A.D. They might have been subjects of the Toltec Empire and therefore would not have arrived until after the eleventh century, or they may have been outcasts, hostile to the Toltec rule, who were pushed south before that date by the expanding dominion of the Empire. The Pipil, then, would be the more probable makers of the Tlaloc effigies."[42]

Since plumbate vessels of the same type have been found under circumstances of greatly varying dates, Vaillant allowed several centuries "for retardations in the civilizations of outlying communities."[43] Therefore, the type which might be dated as of the fifth century at Copán, could conceivably be dated in the eighth or ninth century in peripheral regions.

Referring again to a transitional Type 2-3 frog effigy jar from Copán, Vaillant said: "This change between simple vessels with filleted elements and vessels more pretentiously adapted to the representations of animate forms, we believe to have taken place on the early Toltec horizon, or at least about the seventh century A.D., probably before the entrance of the Pipil in Salvador."[44] Compiling the

41. Vaillant, 1927, pp. 262-263.
42. Vaillant, 1927, p. 261.
43. Vaillant, 1927, p. 260.
44. Vaillant, 1927, p. 274.

QUASI-PLUMBATE EFFIGY VASE *(Tlaloc)*

No. 10/71. *GD.* 13.4. *H.* 17.5. Color: *Cinnamon-Rufous*
(11′ i) *to Hay's Russet* (7′ k).

known data into tabular form, he showed plumbate ware as extending in time from about 450 A.D. until nearly 1200 A.D.[45] This reflected the views of Lothrop, stated above, although some retrenchment was indicated.

Blom and La Farge, in their report of 1927, illustrate a vase with brown metallic glaze from Comitán, Mexico. They say of it: "Pieces with a metallic glaze like this have been found in various parts of the Maya area, chiefly at Copán, and one sherd was found during excavations of the southern Temple of the Ballcourt at Chichén Itzá, showing that this ware was widely distributed by trade. The glaze is accidental, the clay of which the pottery is made containing a slight amount of lead."[46]

From 1927 on, plumbate ware is more and more frequently mentioned in archaeological literature of Middle America. Thompson, in 1929, stated:

A certain type of pottery was made in what is now El Salvador and is easily recognizable because of its glaze, it being the only glazed ware found anywhere in Central America. Pieces of this type have been found in Huehuetenango, Copán, Chichén Itzá, and as far distant as Vera Cruz and Jalisco.[47]

Still interested in the problem of plumbate pottery, Saville, in 1930, pointed out that close relationships must have existed between Guatemala and the Mexican highlands. He said: ". . . we must assume that objects have been exchanged from both directions, having been brought by pilgrims who journeyed southward from Mexico, and by others who went northward from Salvador and Guatemala. In further support of this we need only call attention to the considerable numbers of vases of plumbate ware found at Teotihuacan and other places in central Mexico, which could have originated only in Salvador or

45. Vaillant, 1927, p. 272.
46. Blom & La Farge, 1927, pp. 418-419, fig. 349.
47. Thompson, 1929, pp. 40-44.

PLUMBATE JAR

No. 10/59.   DS. 15.0.   H. 15.3.   Color: *Walnut Brown, some spots of Drab to Grayish Olive, others approaching black* (9″ k grayed, 17‴ to 21‴).

in Guatemala. . . ."[48] This indicates that Saville had, through the years, amended his original idea that plumbate ware originated in the region of Alta Verapaz, Guatemala, to the extent that he considered Salvador also as a possible contributor of this trait.

In the same year, Vaillant, discussing orange "lacquer" ware of Zacatenco, Mexico, said: "The only other locality known to the writer where it is present in quantity is a brickyard in San Juanico . . . associated there with a hard, well kneaded, orange ware . . . with tripod bowls of thick red-on-yellow ware . . . and with plumbate ware."[49]

The Merwin and Vaillant publication of 1932 indicated that definite use of plumbate ware was being made in cross-dating cultural remains. It is stated that no plumbate specimens had then been encountered in either Uaxactun or Holmul, nor had any examples been found in British Honduras. The then known distribution of plumbate pottery is presented briefly. Further light was thrown upon earlier reported finds by Vaillant's work in the valley of Mexico during 1931-1932, which

> showed Plumbate Ware to be absent from the pyramid site of San Juan Teotihuacan but present in a culture found at the adjacent town of San Francisco Mazapan. This Mazapan culture is post-Teotihuacan and pre-Aztec in date, and the ornate Plumbate vessels, figured by Batres (1906 Appendix) and Seler (1915) as coming from Teotihuacan, really belong to this archaeological horizon. On stylistic grounds, the simple Copán forms ought to be earlier than the ornate Teotihuacan examples, but the weakness of Middle American archaeology makes it impossible to correlate chronologically Teotihuacan and the date 9-16-5-0-0 of Stela M.[50]

Contemporaneity of plumbate and fine orange ware on the Isla de Sacrificios; of plumbate, the same type of fine orange, and engraved red ware at Chichén Itzá, where

48. Saville, 1930, p. 206.
49. Vaillant, 1930, p. 43.
50. Merwin & Vaillant, 1932, pp. 79-80.

they occur in the Mexican period; and finally of plumbate with Yucatecan Maya pottery, such as types of carved gray ware, judged late on the Holmul evidence, appears to place all of these wares in "a position coeval with the period of the rise of the Nahua tribes and decline in cultural importance of the Maya groups."[51]

In *Mexico Before Cortez* (1933) Thompson wrote of images of Tlalocs being found all over central and southern Mexico, their worship having extended as far as El Salvador. He added, "In this latter region pottery vessels with a Tlaloc face in relief were manufactured of a lead-bearing clay, and exported far and wide over Central America. . . ."[52] In another place, Thompson had more to say of this ware: ". . . in what is now the Republic of El Salvador a special clay containing a percentage of lead occurs. This when fired acquires a dull metallic lustre varying from blue-green to orange according to the intensity of the firing. . . . Quite apart from the clay, the shapes of the vessels can be recognized as of local patterns, pear-shaped jars, animal forms and vases with heads of the Tlaloc gods predominating. . . . The shapes clearly indicate that the finished vessels, and not the unworked clay, were traded. . . ."[53]

At Chuitinamit, near Lake Atitlan, in Guatemala, Lothrop's excavations yielded only a single sherd of plumbate ware, "part of the rim of a jar with a broad groove just below the lip."[54]

Tozzer, in 1934, when discussing Maya research, commented as follows: "The presence of objects foreign to the places where they are found always raises questions of provenience. The 'plumbate' ware, for example, in all probability made in Salvador, occurs sporadically south-

51. Merwin & Vaillant, 1932, p. 81.
52. Thompson, 1933, p. 141. See Krickeberg, 1933, p. 131.
53. Thompson, 1933, p. 133.
54. Lothrop, 1933, p. 97.

PLUMBATE VASE

No. 10/10. *DS*. 10.0. *H*. 17.7. Color: *Deep Neutral Gray;
one area copper red and iridescent between matte and lus-
trous areas; interior brownish.*

ward in Nicaragua and in the Chiriqui, Panama, and northward in the Ulloa Valley and Copán, Honduras, through the Guatemalan highlands, at Chichén Itzá, Yucatan, in Vera Cruz and in Jalisco, Mexico. The technique is so unusual that a common origin is assumed and many of the specimens must have travelled long distances."[55]

In the same year, Linné brought out his "Archaeological Researches at Teotihuacan," wherein he stated that researches "tend to show that plumbate ware in all probability was unknown to the Teotihuacan culture."[56] Speaking further of this ware, he said:

> A great deal has been written about this exceedingly interesting type of ceramics, and opinions vary considerably. The vessels, which are of thin and hard material, are generally decorated with animal or human figures in relief, separately manufactured and affixed to the ready-formed vessel. . . . Plumbate ware is easily distinguishable from every other kind of pottery, because its surface has a lustre resembling real pottery glaze. . . . From this circumstance the inaccurate appelation of glazed ware has come into being. . . .
> . . . the majority of students seem to be of the opinion that the locality where it was manufactured—provided only one such place existed, and that the Lumholtz type of vessels are imitations—was situated in Salvador. A fair number of this class of vessels have been recovered at Teotihuacan. Strangely enough there are in this case two types, firstly the ordinary, and secondly representations of deities belonging to the Aztec pantheon and in Aztec style. As to the circumstances of their finding, nothing whatever is known.
> Finds have been made, it is true, in a grave at Copán, but opinions seem however inclined to date it to a period following the abandonment of that city. The finds in question do not, moreover, include any Maya vessels. . . . The absence of plumbate ware in

55. Tozzer, 1934, pp. 7-8.
56. Linné, 1934, p. 105.

the Teotihuacan culture . . . points to a comparatively remote antiquity of that civilization.[57]

Vaillant's article, "Chronology and Stratigraphy in the
Maya Area," published in 1935, contains a chart designed
to show how the major ceramic sequences may be tentatively grouped into six periods. His period II, the Mexican Domination Period, is based on the distribution of
plumbate and fine orange ware. In speaking of this period,
Vaillant said:

> The second period, that of Mexican Domination, is
> defined by the presence of Plumbate and Fine Orange
> pottery, which seem to have been distributed during
> the Mexican period at Chichén Itzá. Of the two
> wares, Plumbate is the more important in tracing
> chronological connections between cultures. Its wide
> distribution, due to its apparent commercial desir-
> ability, extends from a probable center in Salvador
> to a northern limit at Tepic and Tula in Mexico to a
> southern one at Tola, Nicaragua. Plumbate ware
> usually occurs under definite time restrictions. To
> date, it has been found in only one stela site, Copán,
> the ceramics of which are closely allied to Salvador.
> On the other hand it is found in the sherd deposits of
> the Mexican period at Chichén Itzá (1200-1458 A. D.—
> f.n. The evaluation of Chilam Balam dates is taken
> from Morley, 1920, 465-535, especially the table on
> 505.)[58] In the Valley of Mexico Plumbate is absent
> in the Teotihuacan culture, but present in the succeed-
> ing Mazapan ceramics. Since Teotihuacan is held to
> have been destroyed in the 11th or 12th centuries, the

57. Linné, 1934, pp. 105-106.

58. Thompson, 1939, p. 234, has said: "Before this Mexican domination, Vaillant places a period of Mexican contact in Yucatan [started
with the conquest of Chichén Itzá by Hunac Ceel in 10.18.10.0.0 (A.D.
1194) and terminated by the overthrow of Mayapan—an important New
Empire Maya city—in Katun 8 Ahau, (11.12.0.0.0; A.D., 1461)—Good-
man-Martinez-Thompson correlation]. According to the writer's ideas
there were two periods of Mexican influence in Yucatan. The first, called
in history the Itza occupation, seemingly lasted from 10.8.0.0.0 (A.D. 987)
to 10.18.10.0.0 (A.D. 1194) when it was terminated by the invasion of
Hunac Ceel, the second extending from that date, as with Vaillant's
Mexican period, to the fall of Mayapan in 11.12.0.0.0 (A.D. 1461)."

occurrence of Plumbate in the Mazapan culture corresponds closely to the time limits imposed by Chichén Itzá.

He further stated, "Both [plumbate and fine orange] wares represent as valid criteria for sequence dating as are provided in Central American ceramics."[59]

The acceptance of plumbate ware as a chronological indicator is illustrated by Roberts' statement, later in 1935, regarding the pottery of the Puuc region: "A factor of importance in the final determination of the position of the sites of the Puuc in the history of the Yucatan-Maya is the *total absence of Plumbate*. This ware has not been found in stratified deposits in any of the Puuc sites."[60]

Strong, the same year, reported the occurrence of one plumbate sherd at site 12, Indian Hill, Bay Islands, Honduras.[61]

In 1936 Lothrop wrote: "In spite of this wide distribution and its easily recognizable character, plumbate is one of the least understood wares and has added to the problems of archaeology rather than aided in their solution."[62] He then presented the following in review:

There are two basic plumbate shapes: (1) subglobular jars with tall necks...; (2) pear-shape jars... These two forms are analogous, the chief difference between them being that the former has a sharp angle where neck meets shoulder, while in the latter neck and shoulder run together without break. These basic shapes are modified by the addition of modeled details which create effigy vessels and at the same time break the external symmetry of outline. Further changes come from the addition of flaring annular bases..., bulbous tripod supports..., or effigy legs... Probably two-thirds of the known plumbate specimens are included in this simple definition of jar types. The remainder consists of bowls or effigy vessels with

59. Vaillant, 1935, p. 121.
60. Roberts, 1935, p. 127. Italics those of the writer.
61. Strong, 1935, pp. 104, 143, 145.
62. Lothrop, 1936, p. 37.

PLUMBATE TRIPOD JAR

No. 10/18. *DS.* 13.6. *H.* 19.0. Color: *Orange-Cinnamon* (13″) *over Cinnamon* (15″) *and Olive Gray* (23′′′′′′ b), *dark olive neck; interior reduced.*

asymmetrical bodies and other forms which do not lend themselves to classification.[63]

Lothrop stated that the source of plumbate ware was still uncertain, with Salvador leading in the number of specimens. He then presented another approach to the point of origin of this ware, namely through style, "for the vessels fall into several definite groups." This is stated thus:

> . . . For instance (1), effigy pots representing certain animals such as the armadillo, jaguar and turkey are always rendered in poses characteristic of Chorotegan polychrome ware as found from Guatemala to Costa Rica. Furthermore (2) there is a class of elongated pear-shaped vessels . . . set on tripods or annular bases, which suggests the local pottery from Vera Cruz in Mexico. . . . In addition (3) there are pots in the form of Tlaloc heads or bearded faces . . . which imply Toltec domination during part of the period of manufacture. Hence the clay beds and center of production must lie in a region subject to these various influences.
>
> The facts set forth in the preceding paragraph give added ground for the belief that plumbate ware originated in central Salvador. Here lived the Maya and the Pipil, the latter being of Toltec extraction, equipped with the religious and artistic traditions to produce the Tlaloc and bearded-head vases. Not far to the east dwelt Chorotega whose influence is attested by trade . . . Between the Chorotega of Nicaragua and Costa Rica and the inhabitants of eastern Mexico there was a stylistic bond in ceramic styles, generally recognized by students but as yet not fully analyzed. Furthermore, a direct connection between central Salvador and eastern Mexico is disclosed by the discovery in the former region of such Mexican objects as stone yokes and paddle stones. . . .[64]

And then Lothrop suggested another alternative, which is as follows:

---

63. Lothrop, 1936, p. 37.
64. Lothrop, 1936, p. 38.

PLUMBATE EFFIGY JAR—ANTHROPOMORPHIC

No. 10/50. *DS.* 12.5. *H.* 15.6. Color: *Light orange, "mud-crack" red; interior reduced except for rim.*

It is considered probable by several students that not only were plumbate vessels passed in trade from a major center of manufacure, but that the actual clay in an unmanufactured state was an article of commerce. If this were true, plumbate vessels must have been made in various localities and their shapes should reflect the point of origin. In addition, we should expect to find vessels made partly of plumbate clay and partly of local clays.[65]

Considering the latter question, he set forth the characteristics of plumbate ware in these words: "The typical vessel of pure plumbate clay is hard, well fired and has a glossy surface which apparently would stand an indefinite amount of use before it was worn away."[66] This is followed by a discussion of vessels which lack both the luster and the hard surface, e. g., specimens from the department of Quiché, in Guatemala, et al. Concerning these it is stated: "Regarded as a group, these vessels appear to be inferior products representing either a blend of clays or defective firing."[67]

As to the other aspect, Lothrop said: "If plumbate clay was traded to be manufactured in various regions, we might expect not only that traditional shapes were copied but that in addition the artistic strain of the locality also would be evident."[68] He has set forth several illustrations where this might be the case. Then he posed the question, "Does this indicate local manufacture or a specialization in production near the source of the clay to supply trade articles especially salable in a given district?"[69]

As has been observed (p. 13), the term *plumbate* has long been in use, but it appears that no explanation of its origin was given until Lothrop, in his 1936 report, wrote: "The color of plumbate ware is usually stated to be that

65. Lothrop, 1936, p. 39.
66. Lothrop, 1936, p. 39.
67. Lothrop, 1936, p. 40.
68. Lothrop, 1936, p. 40.
69. Lothrop, 1936, p. 41.

of lead—whence its name—which changes in whole or in part to orange when fired at high temperatures, or vice versa. So far as we know this is pure surmise based on ocular observation and it remains to be determined what actually happens to plumbate ware in the furnace."[70]

Lothrop pointed out certain characteristic plumbate shapes which were found at Zacualpa in no less than three other colors than those recognized as standard. One is between buff and lemon yellow, another very dark brown comparable to a faded lacquer black ware, and a deep red with black mottlings sharply outlined in vivid orange. Aside from the shapes, these have the other plumbate characteristics of glossy surfaces and incised patterns of decoration. The conclusion regarding these was thus stated: "It seems quite possible that they were made of the usual plumbate clay plus some added ingredient which has changed no feature except the color."[71]

Also included among the Zacualpa pottery is an expression of plumbate ware not previously mentioned. Lothrop said of it, "Another local variation of plumbate ware is crackle. Most examples are completely smooth on the surface, but the specimen in figure 36, *e,* is crackled all over like a true glaze and there is a positive eruption on the neck."[72]

This study of Dr. Lothrop's indicated certain aspects which merited further investigation.

Reporting on the excavations at San José, British Honduras, Thompson said:

> . . . The 1936 excavations . . . produced additional evidence of the far-flung trade relationships of the site

---

70. Lothrop, 1936, p. 41. It is possible that the delay in publishing the reason back of the name *plumbate* may be responsible for the apparent assumption that this ware contained lead, for, according to Webster's unabridged dictionary, "plumbate" means "a salt of plumbic acid." And the definition for "plumbic'" is, "of, pertaining to, like, or containing lead."

71. Lothrop, 1936, p. 41.

72. Lothrop, 1936, p. 41.

during San José V. New examples of Yucatecan slate ware ollas, marble vase fragments and another spindle whorl, decorated with *chapopote* designs in Huaxtec style, were found associated with this phase. The presence of such importations, as well as of carved slate (one example), an apparently early simple silhouette form of orange ware (one example), many finds of carved red ware, and one of copper, together with *total absence of plumbate* and carved orange ware, suggest that San José was abandoned shortly before the Mexican period in Yucatan, but at a time considerably subsequent to 10.3.0.0.0, if San José IV and the transitional phase following it have been correctly placed at the close of Cycle 9.[73]

Wauchope stated that there was an abundance of plumbate ware of several types in the ceramic material from the Zacualpa site, C-II. But "the barranca pottery together with twelve vessels removed from two caches half-way between Groups A and C was quite distinct from that of Group C, the *absence of plumbate ware*, finely (tuff?) tempered orange wares, and animal-head legs, and the occurrence of certain Peten-like shapes and painted decorations suggesting the probability that it was older. . . ." He added further: "In general the pottery gives an impression of lateness, with foreign affiliations chiefly southern."[74]

While carrying on investigations in southern Mexico, E. A. Schumann, Jr., uncovered a plumbate jar which he described thus:

> It is an effigy pot molded to the form of a bird. Its head and tail are missing but its wings are so characteristically molded that its identity is unmistakable. Its similarity with the effigy pottery of ancient Salvador suggests that it may have reached San Gregorio [Chiapas] through a Maya trader.[75]

When Roberts worked over the pottery from Casa Redonda at Chichén Itzá, he found certain negative evidence

---

73. Thompson, 1936, pp. 127-128. Last italics those of the writer.
74. Wauchope, 1936, p. 130. Italics those of the writer.
75. Schumann, 1936, p. 300.

pointing to a period slightly post-dating the period of Mexican occupation of that site. He stated:

> . . . The absence of certain wares from the sherds of the Casa Redonda would argue against the use of the building during the period of Mexican influence or during the period of the actual Mexican occupation of Chichén Itzá. The wares which are most characteristic of these two periods are Fine Orange, Incised Red Ware, *Plumbate* (though not Mexican in origin), and Slate Ware Grater Bowls. No sherds of these wares were found in the collection from the Casa Redonda and their absence in a structure from which the majority of the wares represent types occurring in the late phase of the Mexican occupation period suggests that the particular structure under consideration must have been in use after Chichén Itzá had ceased to be under the domination of Mexican elements, or at least that there had been a cessation of active trade with the peoples in Mexico proper.[76]

In the *History of the Maya*, Gann and Thompson had a few more words regarding the material from which plumbate pottery is made: "In what is to-day the Republic of El Salvador a certain clay, heavily impregnated with lead, was used in making pottery. After firing the vessels assumed a kind of glazed surface, apparently much prized by the different people of Central America. These vessels in certain specialized shapes were exported far and wide."[77]

Dr. Caso, while working in Oaxaca, purchased in Chachuapan a plumbate vase which came from Yucuita. The decoration was in the likeness of a turkey. In Coyotepec he bought a fragment of a plumbate vase, which he identified as being of a very old type.[78] The stratigraphic excavations at Monte Alban, 1936-1937, produced one specimen of plumbate, in the second epoch.[79]

---

76. Roberts, in Pollock, 1937, p. 151. Italics those of the writer.
77. Gann & Thompson, 1937, p. 202.
78. Caso, 1938, p. 54.
79. Caso, 1938, pp. 26 and 31. Dr. Kidder says: "I think this must be a misprint in Caso's publication, as I know he considers that no

Not only scientists, but non-scientific writers as well have given attention to this class of ceramics. For instance, Helen E. Stiles refers to it thus:

> In Guatemala and western Salvador prehistoric pottery has been found which has a so-called semi-glaze. Lead in the clay caused this effect when the pottery was fired. The Indians learned to use this particular clay for an interesting ware which they decorated with modeled forms and incised lines.[80]

Karl Ruppert has reported that "among sherds excavated at Los Tuxtlas [Ver.] in 1939 were a few in all probability from plumbate vessels."[81]

Vaillant, in his correlations in the valley of Mexico, 1938, wrote of the site, Tenenepango, as producing vessels in plaster cloisonné as well as of the orange-on-white matte lacquer type of Mazapan, and added: "Plumbate ware and Mazapan tripod thick line red-on-yellow bind these wares into the Chichimec period (which is found lying above Teotihuacan remains or below those of Aztec date, or which can be tied in through trade wares to material so defined by stratigraphical method)."[82] He dates the Chichimec period in the valley of Mexico, 1100-1300 A.D.[83]

While the present paper was being written, *The Maya and Their Neighbors* was released from press. Thompson, in discussing the "Problems of the Lowland Maya," said of the eastern British Honduras sites: "The *absence of plumbate* and typical fine orange pottery, turquoise and gold . . . hint that these sites are not contemporaneous with the Mexican period in Yucatan."[84]

---

plumbate appeared at Monte Alban until Period IV." Letter, 8-5-42. However, Dr. Caso, in reading this manuscript, made no comment thereon.

---

80. Stiles, 1939, p. 119. This illustrates the importance of making exhaustive studies of material before publishing information thereon.

81. Thompson, 1941, p. 64.

82. Vaillant, 1938, p. 545.

83. Vaillant, 1938, p. 545.

84. Thompson, 1940, p. 129. Italics those of the writer.

Mary Butler, writing of the material from ruins at Chamá and Chipal, in the departments of Alta Verapaz and Quiché, respectively, of Guatemala, spoke of plumbate as "a distinctive ware apparently exported north from Salvador relatively late in pre-historic times." The pottery groups which she designates as Chipal 1 *lack plumbate ware*. Her Chipal 2, which ushers in a new period, sees a "wave of new influence in the Chixoy drainage in which emphasis in pottery is laid on texture and shape rather than on decoration. Effigy, except in Plumbate Ware, is confined to applied decoration, becomes stylized, and tends to crudity and vigor rather than fine representation. The contemporary appearance of fine effigy in Plumbate supports the suggestion that this ware comes from a southern periphery of the Maya area presumably reached late by fine style influence. Plumbate and Fine Orange Wares, characteristic of the period, tie in to the late phase of Maya history through their association with the Mexican period in Yucatan." A final period, indicated as Chipal 3, has been tentatively established, which is defined primarily by negative evidence, "the lack of metal in the Plumbate Period and the *lack of Plumbate*. . . . "[85]

From the closely paralleled distribution of plumbate ware "from the south," and fine orange "from the north," with the type of ceremonialism represented by the fifth period at Monte Alban—the closely unified religious system of the Mixteca-Puebla culture—Vaillant now perceives very important implications. He has said: "Four things are notable about the Mixteca-Puebla culture: its spread is shown mainly in terms of ritualistic presentation; there is evidence that much of the distribution was accomplished by movements of peoples; the movement seems datable as between 1100-1300; at Monte Alban and at Teotihuacan, this complex replaced in the first case directly and in the second case indirectly, stable individualized local cul-

---

85. Butler, 1940, pp. 260, 262, and 265. Italics those of the writer.

tures."[86] In a comparative table (XI) of New World ceramic sequences, he has placed the Mazapan period, in which plumbate and fine orange wares occur, about A. D. 1100.[87]

Wauchope, in his 1941 publication,[88] mentioned again the plumbate finds at Zacualpa. Thompson, in the same year, made the statement that, "Plumbate pottery has been satisfactorily placed on the Mazapan-Mexican Chichen Itza (A.D. 1100-1450) horizon, but it is worthy of note that present evidence now tends to place its center of manufacture in or near western Guatemala, yet the considerable number of plumbate vessels with Tlaloc features would argue against a Maya origin, unless one is prepared to accept the unlikely assumption that Maya potters deliberately catered for foreign markets by decorating their products with the features of the importers' chief god. Possibly Zoque-Mixe or Nahua-speaking peoples of eastern Chiapas produced this interesting ware. Representations of tapirs suggest a lowland area or its vicinity."[89]

It is now to be noted that plumbate ware has been assigned to a period of comparatively short duration—quite in contrast with views expressed earlier in this paper.

Valenzuela has reported finds of plumbate ware at Mixtan and Playa Vicente, Oaxaca.[90]

From reports made, and the discussions which followed them, at the *Primera Sesión de la Mesa Redonda sobre Problemas Antropológicos Mexicanos y Centro Americanos*, in Mexico City, July 11-14, 1941, several points regarding plumbate pottery may be added. The recent excavations at Tula, Hidalgo, have shown that plumbate ware is present in all the culture levels, with more specimens near the surface than lower down.[91] At the site of Huapalcalco,

---

86. Vaillant, 1940, pp. 299-300.
87. Vaillant, 1940, p. 488.
88. Wauchope, 1941, p. 212 ff.
89. Thompson, 1941, p. 42.
90. Valenzuela, 1941, Ms.
91. See also: Acosta, 1940, p. 176 ff.

near Tula, a considerable amount of plumbate ware has been found. Phase V at Teotihuacan has produced some plumbate ware.

At Monte Alban very few plumbate sherds have been found, but some plumbate vessels have been recovered from phase IV. Two jars from Texmilincan, Guerrero, were found in a tomb by Sr. Sidonio Moreno, associated with copper, a pyrite mirror, fine orange, and a piece of gold. The culture is Mixtec.

Vaillant, in a 1941 publication, discussing the pottery traded by the Mazapeños, said: " . . . the Mazapan peoples received pottery from distant sources. From Puebla and Vera Cruz they acquired a popular fine orange ware . . . They had also the distinctive pseudo-vitreous ware called plumbate, which had a wide orbit of commercial distribution. . . . This ware is never found in classical Maya centers but appears in the later sites. In the Valley of Mexico it never reached the Teotihuacan Toltec, and its distribution ceased in Aztec times."[92] As has been shown above, he has dated Mazapan culture about A.D. 1100-1300.

In another work of the same year, Vaillant summarized the plumbate and fine orange ware situation as follows:

Both these wares seem confined to a short period, which is sharply defined. They do not appear in the Petén. In the Alta Verapaz and probably Yucatán they succeed picture painted vases. In Yucatán Fine Orange and Plumbate are associated with the Mexican occupation at the close of the Twelfth Century. In Oaxaca, the two wares appear at the end of Period IV or the beginning of Period V, when Mixteca-Puebla influence transformed the Zapotec ceremonial culture. In the Valley of Mexico these two wares came after the abandonment of Toltec Teotihuacan and Azcapotzalco, and are associated with the Mazapan culture which antedated the spread of Aztec II-IV wares almost certainly datable at 1300-1520. At Cholula Plumbate and Fine Orange occur after the Teotihuacan occupation but prior to the rise of sophisticated Puebla poly-

92. Vaillant, 1941, p. 78.

QUASI-PLUMBATE BOWL WITH ANNULAR BASE

No. 10/11. DO. 13.2. H. 5.7. Color: *Bright orange with a little Apricot Orange (11')*

chrome; and in Vera Cruz these wares are associable with the Cerro Montoso culture, which succeeded Ranchito de las Animas. Only at Copán in Honduras is there evidence of an earlier origin for Plumbate.[93]

Brainerd, also in 1941, speaking of the association of fine orange and plumbate pottery at Chichén Itzá, said: "Shapes and designs on X fine orange and plumbate are obviously related.[94] . . . The site or area in which X fine orange was made must be contemporaneous with plumbate and probably with Cerro Montoso polychrome; that is, in the Mazapan-Chichimec-Monte Alban IIIc-Aztec I horizon according to the consensus of opinion among specialists in Mexican archaeology.[95]

Throughout the works of recent years, it is seen that there are certain culture traits (plumbate, fine orange, copper bells, gold ornaments, tecali vessels, pyrite mirrors, specially made spindle whorls, etc.) that form a flocculation which, in turn, is assigned to a certain period of time. This has been primarily determined from evidence

---

93. Vaillant, 1941a, p. 240.

As would be expected, additional excavations at Copán have indicated that all plumbate ware from that site belongs to a period post-dating its major occupation. This fact is revealed by Dr. Kidder, who states: "The situation regarding plumbate at Copan has been somewhat clarified by Stromsvik's recent excavations. We know nothing about the circumstances of the finding of the Peabody Museum specimens, and their discovery at Copan led Lothrop and Vaillant to give plumbate a considerably greater chronological range than now seems justifiable. I think there can be little doubt that all plumbate at Copan is subsequent to the major occupation of the site, as in all Stromsvik's excavations no single sherd has been found save in superficial deposits. One sherd came to light in material accumulated in one of the ball court temples after the roof had fallen; and a vessel was found in a grave sunk into the ruins of a chamber in the south end of the Court of the Hieroglyphic Stairway." Kidder, Letter, 8-5-42.

Stromsvik himself adds: "What little plumbate has been found at Copan hails from what we call post-occupation period, or after the end of the 10th cycle (10.0.0.0.0, or about 830 A. D., Goodman-Thompson-Martinez correlation)." Letter 8-20-42.

94. Brainerd, 1941, p. 178.

95. Brainerd, 1941, p. 181.

of the Mexican occupation of Chichén Itzá and the dating
of plumbate ware in the Valley of Mexico. Then from
various areas, the occurrence of these traits has been relatively dated. The whole thing rests on the dates given to
this block of traits. And how this may be fitted into two
chronological schemes has now been demonstrated by
Eric Thompson, who, in his most recent publication, has
stated: "There is . . . a not inconsiderable body of evidence that plumbate and the local forms of fine orange
were in use at Chichen Itza up to the time of its abandonment, but when did this abandonment take place?"[96]

He then proceeds to show how events led to the abandonment of Chichén Itzá, not at the time of the fall of Mayapan (1441), but over two hundred years prior to that, in
1204. He stresses the fact that: "This whole question of
the abandonment of Chichen Itza is of vital importance in
dating the Mexican period at Chichen Itza, and also for
dating plumbate and the types of fine orange under discussion. In the one case plumbate would have lasted until
A.D. 1441 (Scheme A). In the other case it endured until
A.D. 1204 (Scheme B). . . . "[97]

According to Thompson, "all authorities agree that
Early Mazapan ended not later than A.D. 1240 and Aztec
I not later than A.D. 1300. That is, plumbate vanishes in
Central Mexico one hundred and fifty to two hundred years
before the fall of Mayapan. . . . Since the periods following
the disappearance of plumbate were marked by augment-
ing commerce, one must conclude that its subsequent
absence from Central Mexico was due to the fact that it
was not manufactured after the Mazapan period. In that
case Chichen Itza was abandoned not at the time of the fall
of Mayapan (A.D. 1441), but at the time of the Hunac
Ceel incident (A.D. 1184-1204), the latter event coinciding
with the plumbate period in Central Mexico according to

---

96. Thompson, 1941a, p. 100.
97. Thompson, 1941a, p. 101.

the Vaillant reconstruction and with Aztec I according to the Caso scheme."[98]

In concluding this study, Thompson has said:

> The abandonment of Chichen Itza at the time of the Hunac Ceel incident (A.D. 1184-1204) cannot, of course, be considered as definitely proved, but the Roys scheme [B], now buttressed by archaeological evidence, appears to be the best means of reconciling what otherwise would be very conflicting conclusions from Central Mexico and Chichen Itza respectively. Such a reconstruction also diminishes the lacuna between the pottery of the final periods of Uaxactun and San Jose on the one hand and the plumbate horizon on the other. The narrow gap still remaining is probably filled by the carved slate horizon, for . . . the examples of Yucatecan slate ware found on the surface at San Jose, and therefore from the final stage of occupation or even deposited in a reoccupation, typologically fit best in the pre-plumbate Puuc horizon. This reconstruction, if correct, would invalidate the 11.3.0.0.0 correlation, for under such a correlation plumbate would coincide with the Old Empire. It would also push back to A.D. 1000-1250 approximately the flocculation recently proposed by me.[99]

Thompson added a postscript to his paper, stating: "The term *plumbate* and *plumbate pottery*, as used in this article should be read as having reference only to the more elaborate vessels, usually in effigy form, which were widely traded [around A.D. 1000].[100] There are some grounds for believing that certain simple forms of plumbate pottery, notably a plain cylindrical jar, may have been made at an earlier date, but probably were traded only within southern and central Guatemala and immediately adjacent regions."[101]

Comparing the Tajumulco plumbate vessels with examples from Kaminaljuyú, El Baul, and San Augustin

---

98. Thompson, 1941a, pp. 102-103.
99. Thompson, 1941a, p.109.
100. Thompson, Letter, 8-18-42.
101. Thompson, 1941a, p. 109.

Acasaguastlan, Thompson suggests the dates of about A.D. 1000-1250 for Tajumulco.[102]   And the simplest forms indicate that Tajumulco's beginning might be a hundred years earlier.   Furthermore, Thompson looks upon these plain domestic types as "indications that Tajumulco is not far distant from the center of manufacture of this ware,"[103] and he states that "it is more reasonable to suppose that plumbate was manfactured by some community in southeastern Chiapas. . . . "[104]

This, then, brings up-to-date the subject of plumbate history. It reveals the fact that for over one hundred years people have been writing about a particular type of pottery; some general characteristics have been accepted, but no one has set forth a comprehensive description and analysis of what plumbate pottery actually is;[105] certain students have argued that the ware has a true glaze, while others have disputed that view; very wide distribution has been revealed; gradually the time span has been reduced, and plumbate pottery has been relegated to a period of about three hundred and fifty years' duration (A.D. 900-1250 according to one scheme, 1100-1450 according to another) ; the ware has been determined as a non-Maya trait, and strong Toltec implications have been recognized; but, as yet, no one has ascertained the exact source, or sources, of this abundant ware.   Clearly, technical studies are required to supplement the contributions of the field archaeologist; and specific investigations will have to be carried out before the plumbate problem can be satisfactorily settled.   It is hoped that the Tajumulco specimens may shed additional light on this subject.

---

102. Thompson, Letter, 8-18-42.
103. Thompson, 1941a, p. 97.
104. Thompson, 1941a, p. 98.
105. Except for a specimen from Tepic, Mexico, which Lumholtz had analyzed. *See:* p. 7.

REFERENCES CITED

Acosta, J. R.
    1940   Exploraciones en Tula, Hgo., 1940. Revista Mexicana de
           Estudios Antropológicos, tom. 4, no. 3, pp. 172-194. Mexico.

Batres, L.
    1906   Teotihuacan. Memoria que presenta Leopoldo Batres al XV
           Congresa Internacional de Americanistas, Quebec, 1906.
           Mexico.

Blom, F. and O. La Farge II
    1927   Tribes and Temples. *Middle Amer. research ser.*, pub. no. 1,
           vol. 2. Dept. Middle Amer. Research, Tulane Univ. New
           Orleans.

Brainerd, G. W.
    1941   Fine Orange Pottery in Yucatan. Revista Mexicana de
           Estudios Anthropológicos, tom. 5, nos. 2-3, pp. 163-182.
           Mexico.

Butler [Lewis], M.
    1940   A Pottery Sequence from Guatemala. *The Maya and Their
           Neighbors*, pp. 250-267. New York.

Carnegie Institution of Washington News Service Bulletin
    1936   Important Maya Discovery in the Guatemalan Highlands.
           Carnegie Inst. Wash. news serv. bull., vol. 4, no. 6, pp. 55-60,
           August 23. Washington.

Carrillo y Ancona, C.
    1885   Los Cabezas-Chatas. *An. Mus. Nac. Mex.*, tom. 3, entrega 7.
           Mexico.

Caso, A.
    1938   Exploraciones en Oaxaca, quinta y sexta temporadas 1936-
           1937. *Inst. Pan-Am. Geog. e Hist.*, pub. no. 34. Mexico.

Charnay, D.
    1887   The Ancient Cities of the New World. New York.

Gann, T. and J. E. S. Thompson
    1937   The History of the Maya. New York.

Joyce, T. A.
    1914   Mexican Archaeology. New York.

Krickeberg, W.
    1933   Los Totonaca. Contribución a la Etnografía Histórica de la
           América Central. Secretaría de Educación Pública. Mexico.

Linné, S.
    1934   Archaeological Researches at Teotihuacan, Mexico. *Ethnol.
           Mus. of Sweden*, n. s., pub. no. 1. Stockholm.

Lothrop, S. K.
    1926   Pottery of Costa Rica and Nicaragua. *Contr. Mus. Amer.
           Ind.*, Heye Found., vol. 8, vol. 1, New York.

1927 The Museum Central American Expedition, 1925-1926. *Ind. Notes, Mus. Amer. Ind.*, Heye Found., vol. 4, no. 1, pp. 12-33. New York.

1927a Pottery Types and Their Sequence in El Salvador. *Ind. Notes and Monog., Mus. Amer. Ind.*, Heye Found., vol. 1, no. 4, pp. 165-218. New York.

1933 Atitlan, an Archaeological Study of Ancient Remains on the Borders of Lake Atitian, Guatemala. *Carnegie Inst. Wash.* pub. no. 444. Washington.

1936 Zacualpa, a Study of Ancient Quiche Artifacts. *Carnegie Inst. Wash.* pub. no. 472. Washington.

Lumholtz, C.

1902 Unknown Mexico. vol. 2. New York.

Merwin, R. E. and G. C. Vaillant.

1932 The Ruins of Holmul, Guatemala. *Mem. Peabody Mus. Amer. Archaeol. and Ethnol.*, Harvard Univ., vol. 3, no. 2. Cambridge.

Pollock, H. E. D.

1937 The Casa Redonda at Chichen Itza, Yucatan. *Carnegie Inst. Wash.* pub. no. 456, pp. 131-154. Washington.

Roberts, H. B.

1935 Ceramics. *Carnegie Inst. Wash. year book*, no. 34, pp. 126-127. Washington.

Ruppert, K.

1935 The Caracol at Chichen Itza, Yucatan, Mexico. *Carnegie Inst. Wash.* pub. no. 454. Washington.

Saville, M. H.

1916 The Glazed Ware of Central America, with Special Reference to a Whistling Jar from Honduras. *Holmes anniv. vol.*, pp. 421-426. Washington.

1930 Toltec or Teotihuacan Types of Artifacts in Guatemala. *Ind. Notes, Mus. Amer. Ind.*, Heye Found., vol. 7, no. 2, pp. 195-206. New York.

Schumann, E. A. Jr.

1936 A Recent Visit to Southern Mexico. *Maya research*, vol. 3, nos. 3-4., pp. 296-305. New Orleans.

Seler, E.

1904 Antiquities of Guatemala. *Bur. Amer. Ethnol.*, bull. 28, pp. 77-121. Washington.

1915 Die Teotiuacan-Kultur des Hochlands von México. *Gesammelte Abhandlungen*, band 5. Berlin.

Seler-Sachs, C.

1922 Altertümer des Kanton Tuxtla im Staate Veracruz. *Festschrift Eduard Seler*. Stuttgart.

Spinden, H. J.
1915 Notes on the Archaeology of Salvador. *Amer. anthropologist*, n. s., vol. 17, no. 3, pp. 446-484. Lancaster.

Stiles, H. E.
1939 Pottery of the American Indians. New York.

Strong, W. D.
1935 Archaeological Investigations in the Bay Islands, Spanish Honduras. *Smithsonian Inst. misc. coll.*, vol. 92, no. 14. Washington.

Thompson, J. E. S.
1929 Comunicaciones y Comercio de los Antiguos Mayas. *An. Soc. Geog. e Hist. Guat.*, tom. 2, Sept. 1929, pp. 40-44. Guatemala City.

1933 Mexico Before Cortez. New York.

1936 Exploration in Campeche and Quintana Roo and Excavations at San Jose, British Honduras. *Carnegie Inst. Wash. year book*, no. 35, pp. 125-128. Washington.

1939 Excavations at San Jose, British Honduras. *Carnegie Inst. Wash.* pub. no. 506. Washington.

1940 Archaeological Problems of the Lowland Maya. *The Maya and Their Neighbors*, pp. 126-138. New York.

1941 Dating of Certain Inscriptions of non-Maya Origin. *Carnegie Inst. Wash.* theoretical approaches to problems, no. 1. Washington.

1941a A Coordination of the History of Chichen Itza with Ceramic Sequences in Central Mexico. *Revista Mex. Estud. Antro.*, tom. 5, nos. 2-3, pp. 97-109. Mexico.

Thompson, J. E. S. and F. B. Richardson (editors)
1939 Gesammelte Abhandlungen zur Amerikanischen Sprach- und Alter-Thumskunde, vols. I-V, by Edward Seler, Berlin, 1902-1923. English translation, vol. V, no. 14. *Carnegie Inst. Wash.* Cambridge.

Tozzer, A. M.
1934 Maya Research. *Maya research*, vol. 1, no. 1, pp. 3-19. New York.

Valenzuela, J.
1941 Breve informe de las exploraciones y reconido que practicamos al sur de Veracruz comprendiendo al efecto varios lugares de las cuencas del Rio Tesichuacan y la pirámide del castillo en Tuxtepec, Oax. *Ms.* Mexico.

Vaillant, G. C.
1926 Quoted in S. G. Morley, *Carnegie Inst. Wash. year book* no. 25, pp. 271-273.

1927   The Chronological Significance of Maya Ceramics. *Ms., Peabody Mus. Amer. Archaeol. and Ethnol.*, Harvard Univ. Cambridge.

1930   Excavations at Zacatenco. *Anthro. papers, Amer. Mus. Nat. Hist.*, vol. 32, pt. 1. New York.

1935   Chronology and Stratigraphy in the Maya Area. *Maya research*, vol. 2, pp. 119-139. New York.

1938   A Correlation of Archaeological and Historical Sequences in the Valley of Mexico. *Amer. anthropologist*, n. s., vol. 40, no. 4, pp. 535-573. Menasha.

1940   Patterns in Middle American Archaeology. *The Maya and Their Neighbors*, pp. 295-305. New York.

1941   Aztecs of Mexico. Garden City, N. Y.

Wauchope, R.

1936   Zacualpa. *Carnegie Inst. Wash. year book* no. 35, pp. 128-130. Washington.

1941   Effigy Head Vessel Supports from Zacualpa, Guatemala. *Los Mayas Antiguos*, pp. 211-231. Mexico.